meals in minutes
slow cooker

RECIPES
Norman Kolpas

PHOTOGRAPHS
Bill Bettencourt

weldon**owen**

contents

15 MINUTES HANDS-ON TIME

about this book

At first a slow cooker book that purports to help you make food quickly may seem like a contradiction in terms. But while it's true that the start-to-finish cooking times are quite long, slow cookers are actually ideal time-saving tools for busy cooks. Once the ingredients are prepared and placed in the cooker, they require no further attention until you arrive home after a long day, ready to serve up a hot meal.

With a slow cooker, even deeply flavored one-pot meals like Chicken Cacciatore, Ale-Braised Short Ribs, and Osso Buco with Mushrooms and Peas don't have to involve a lot of work. In fact, all of the recipes in this book require less than 30 minutes of hands-on prep time—many of them less than 15 minutes. Add a green salad, and you have a nourishing home-cooked meal that demands surprisingly little effort to put on the table.

15 minutes
hands-on time

tuscan
ribollita

Dried cannellini beans,
1 lb (500 g), picked over

Olive oil, ¼ cup (2 fl oz/
60 ml), plus more for drizzling

Yellow onions, 2, chopped

Garlic, 2 cloves, minced

Tomato paste, ¼ cup
(2 oz/60 g)

**Vegetable or chicken
broth,** 8 cups (64 fl oz/2 l)

Kale or savoy cabbage,
1 bunch (about 1 lb/500 g),
coarsely chopped

Carrots, 4, coarsely chopped

Celery, 2 stalks, coarsely
chopped

Fresh thyme, 1 tablespoon
minced

**Salt and freshly ground
pepper**

Day-old country bread,
3 cups (6 oz/185 g) cubed

SERVES 6–8

1 Soak the beans

In a large bowl, soak the beans in cold water to cover for at least 8 hours or for up to overnight. Alternatively, put the beans in a large saucepan with cold water to cover. Bring to a boil over high heat. Remove from the heat and let sit, covered, for 1 hour. Drain the beans and set aside.

2 Sauté the vegetables

In a frying pan over medium heat, warm the ¼ cup olive oil. Add the onions and garlic and sauté until softened, about 5 minutes. Add the tomato paste and sauté until it darkens, about 2 minutes longer. Pour in the broth, raise the heat to high, and bring to a boil. Remove from the heat.

3 Cook the soup

Put the drained beans, kale, carrots, celery, and thyme in the slow cooker and sprinkle with 2 teaspoons salt and 1 teaspoon pepper. Pour in the broth mixture. Cover and cook on the high-heat setting for 4 hours or the low-heat setting for 8 hours. About 10 minutes before the soup is ready, stir in the bread cubes, cover, and continue cooking. When the soup is ready, season to taste with salt and pepper. Ladle into bowls and serve, passing additional olive oil at the table.

cook's tip

To save time, substitute 6 cups (48 oz/1.5 kg) canned beans, drained and rinsed, for the dried beans. Add to the *ribollita* along with the bread cubes in step 3.

cook's tip

For a complete meal, serve the
curry over steamed long-grain
white rice such as basmati.
Accompany with a fresh tomato
and cucumber salad drizzled
with plain yogurt and sprinkled
with chopped fresh cilantro
(fresh coriander).

indian vegetable curry

1 **Sauté the vegetables and spices**
In a frying pan over medium-high heat, warm the oil. Add the onions and garlic and sauté until softened, about 5 minutes. Add the ginger, coriander, turmeric, and cumin seeds and sauté until fragrant, about 1 minute. Add 1 cup (8 fl oz/ 250 ml) hot water and deglaze the pan, stirring to scrape up the browned bits on the pan bottom. When the water comes to a boil, remove the pan from the heat.

2 **Cook the curry**
Put the potatoes, cauliflower, and green beans in the slow cooker. Pour the contents of the frying pan over them. Sprinkle with 1½ teaspoons salt and stir to combine. Cover and cook on the high-heat setting for 4 hours or the low-heat setting for 8 hours. Add the cilantro and stir to combine. Season to taste with salt, and serve.

Canola oil, ¼ cup (2 fl oz/60 ml)

Yellow onions, 2, chopped

Garlic, 4 cloves, minced

Fresh ginger, 3 tablespoons minced

Ground coriander, 1½ teaspoons

Ground turmeric, 1 teaspoon

Cumin seeds, 1 teaspoon

Boiling potatoes, 1 lb (500 g), peeled and cut into chunks

Cauliflower, 1 large head, trimmed and cut into florets

Green beans, ¾ lb (375 g), trimmed and coarsely chopped

Salt

Fresh cilantro (fresh coriander), ¼ cup (⅓ oz/ 10 g) chopped

SERVES 6–8

chicken adobo

Yellow onions, 4, halved and sliced

Garlic, 4 cloves, crushed

Bay leaf, 1

Black peppercorns, 1 teaspoon

Skinless chicken thighs, 8, about 3 lb (1.5 kg) total weight, trimmed of excess fat

Rice vinegar, ½ cup (4 fl oz/125 ml)

Soy sauce, ½ cup (4 fl oz/ 125 ml), plus more for serving

Sugar, 1 tablespoon

Steamed white rice, for serving

SERVES 8

1 **Assemble the adobo**
Spread half of the sliced onions in the bottom of the slow cooker. Add 2 of the garlic cloves, the bay leaf, and the peppercorns. Arrange the chicken in a single layer on top of the onions. Top with the remaining onions and garlic. Drizzle the vinegar and soy sauce over the ingredients and sprinkle with the sugar.

2 **Cook the adobo**
Cover and cook on the high-heat setting for 4 hours or the low-heat setting for 8 hours. Remove and discard the bay leaf. Divide the steamed rice among 8 plates and top with the chicken. Spoon the juices from the slow cooker on top and serve, passing additional soy sauce at the table.

cook's tip

For a variation on this savory
Philippine dish, instead of
chicken, use 3 lb (1.5 kg) beef
stew meat or lean pork, cut
into 1½-inch (4-cm) chunks.

cook's tip

Serve this Italian classic over
fresh egg noodles or strand
pasta, such as fettuccine (shown
above) or pappardelle, to soak
up all the juices.

chicken
cacciatore

1 Brown the chicken

On a large plate, stir together the flour, 1 tablespoon salt, and 1½ teaspoons pepper. Coat the chicken pieces evenly with the flour mixture, shaking off the excess. In a large frying pan over medium-high heat, warm the oil. Add the chicken pieces, in batches if necessary, skin side down, and cook until golden brown on the bottom, about 7 minutes. Turn the chicken and cook on the second side until lightly browned, 3–4 minutes longer. Transfer the chicken pieces to the slow cooker.

2 Cook the chicken and vegetables

Return the frying pan to medium-high heat. Add the bell peppers, onion, and garlic and sauté until they start to soften, about 3 minutes. Pour in the wine and broth, and deglaze the pan, stirring to scrape up the browned bits on the pan bottom. Stir in the tomatoes and oregano and bring to a simmer. Pour the mixture over the chicken. Cover and cook on the high-heat setting for 4 hours or the low-heat setting for 8 hours.

3 Add the mushrooms

About 10 minutes before the dish is ready, stir in the mushrooms. Season to taste with salt and pepper and serve.

Flour, ⅓ cup (2 oz/60 g)

Salt and freshly ground pepper

Whole chicken, 3½–4 lb (1.75–2 kg), cut into 8 serving pieces

Olive oil, ¼ cup (2 fl oz/ 60 ml)

Red or yellow bell peppers (capsicums), 2, sliced

Yellow onion, 1, halved and sliced

Garlic, 4 cloves, minced

Dry red wine, ¾ cup (6 fl oz/180 ml)

Chicken broth, ¾ cup (6 fl oz/180 ml)

Crushed plum (Roma) tomatoes, 1 can (28 oz/ 875 g)

Dried oregano, 1 tablespoon

Button or cremini mushrooms, 6 oz (185 g), sliced

SERVES 6

braised duck with figs & port

Duck legs, 6, about 4 lb (2 kg) total weight

Salt and freshly ground pepper

Unsalted butter, 3 tablespoons

Olive oil, 3 tablespoons

Yellow onion, 1, finely chopped

Garlic, 3 cloves, minced

Port wine, 1 cup (8 fl oz/ 250 ml)

Chicken broth, ¾ cup (6 fl oz/180 ml)

Fresh thyme, 3 sprigs

Dried figs, 2 cups (¾ lb/375 g)

SERVES 6

1 **Brown the duck**
Season the duck legs on both sides with salt and pepper. In a large frying pan over medium-high heat, melt the butter with the oil. Add the onion and garlic and sauté until they start to soften, about 4 minutes. Push the onion and garlic to the side of the pan and place the duck legs, skin side down, in the center. Cook until golden brown on the bottom, about 5 minutes. Turn the legs over and cook until browned on the second side, about 3 minutes. Transfer the duck legs, skin side up, to the slow cooker.

2 **Cook the duck**
Return the frying pan with the onion and garlic to medium-high heat. Pour in the port and broth and deglaze the pan, stirring to scrape up the browned bits on the pan bottom. Bring to a boil, then pour into the slow cooker. Add the thyme sprigs and figs. Cover and cook on the high-heat setting for 3½ hours or the low-heat setting for 7 hours.

3 **Finish the dish**
Remove and discard the thyme sprigs. Transfer the duck legs to a platter and let them sit, covered loosely with aluminum foil, for about 10 minutes. Skim off and discard most of the fat from the surface of the cooking liquid. Season the liquid to taste with salt and pepper. Divide the legs among 6 plates, spoon the juices and figs on top, and serve.

cook's tip

To store any leftover duck, remove the meat from the bones, discarding the skin. Shred the meat and store in an airtight container in the refrigerator for up to 2 days. When ready to serve, reheat the meat in the sauce and serve over wide egg noodles or panfried potatoes for a quick and easy main dish.

cook's tip

Chile verde makes a great filling for burritos: place a large spoonful of pork and steamed rice down the center of a warmed flour tortilla. Sprinkle with shredded cheese and shredded lettuce, then drizzle with sour cream. Fold in both sides and roll up into a burrito.

chile
verde

1 Cook the stew
Put the chiles and their liquid in the slow cooker, tearing the chiles into coarse strips with your fingers. Stir in the pork, chicken broth, garlic, oregano, 1½ teaspoons salt, and ½ teaspoon white pepper. Cover and cook on the high-heat setting for 4 hours or the low-heat setting for 8 hours.

2 Serve and garnish the stew
Taste and adjust the seasoning. Ladle the stew over steamed rice and serve, passing the sour cream and cilantro at the table.

Canned roasted whole green chiles, 8 oz (250 g)

Boneless pork shoulder, 3 lb (1.5 kg), cut into 1-inch (2.5-cm) cubes

Chicken broth, 2 cups (16 fl oz/500 ml)

Garlic, 4 cloves, minced

Dried oregano, 1 teaspoon

Salt and ground white pepper

Steamed white rice, for serving

Sour cream, ¾ cup (6 oz/185 g)

Fresh cilantro (fresh coriander), ½ cup (¾ oz/ 20 g) chopped

SERVES 6–8

spring veal stew

Boneless veal shank or shoulder, 3 lb (1.5 kg), cut into 2-inch (5-cm) cubes

Salt and freshly ground pepper

Unsalted butter, 3 tablespoons

Olive oil, 3 tablespoons

Leeks, 2, white and pale green parts, halved, rinsed, and thinly sliced

Dry white wine, 1 cup (8 fl oz/250 ml)

Fresh thyme, 2 sprigs

Asparagus, ½ lb (250 g), tough ends removed and coarsely chopped

Button or cremini mushrooms, 6 oz (185 g), sliced

Frozen peas, ½ lb (250 g)

Crème fraîche or sour cream, ½ cup (4 oz/125 g)

Fresh flat-leaf (Italian) parsley, 3 tablespoons chopped

SERVES 6–8

1 Brown the veal

Season the veal cubes with salt and pepper. In a large frying pan over medium-high heat, melt the butter with the oil. Add the veal and cook, in batches if necessary to avoid crowding, until golden brown on all sides, 7–10 minutes total. Add the leeks and sauté until they start to soften, about 3 minutes longer. Transfer the veal and leeks to the slow cooker.

2 Cook the stew

Return the pan to medium-high heat, add the wine, and deglaze the pan, stirring to scrape up the browned bits on the pan bottom. Bring the wine to a boil and pour over the veal. Add the thyme sprigs, cover, and cook on the high-heat setting for 3 hours or the low-heat setting for 6–6½ hours.

3 Add the vegetables

Add the asparagus, mushrooms, and peas and stir to combine. Cover and continue cooking until the vegetables are tender, 20–30 minutes. Remove and discard the thyme sprigs. Stir in the crème fraîche until it is blended with the cooking juices. Season to taste with salt and pepper. Spoon the stew into shallow bowls, garnish with the parsley, and serve.

cook's tip

If the season is right and fresh peas are available, substitute 2 lb (1 kg) peas in the pod for the frozen peas. Shell them and add to the stew in step 3.

cook's tip

Coconut milk, an essential ingredient in Southeast Asian cooking, is used in a broad range of dishes from curries to soups. Before opening a can of coconut milk, shake it well to blend the milk and cream.

indonesian
beef stew

1 Sauté the beef
In a large frying pan over medium-high heat, warm the oil. Add the beef and onion and cook, stirring frequently, until the meat is no longer red and the onion has softened, about 4 minutes. Sprinkle with the shredded coconut, brown sugar, coriander, cumin, and 1 teaspoon each salt and pepper. Continue sautéing until the meat and coconut are browned and the spices are fragrant, 5–7 minutes longer. Transfer the mixture to the slow cooker.

2 Cook the stew
Add the coconut milk to the frying pan, raise the heat to high, and deglaze the pan, stirring to scrape up the browned bits on the pan bottom. Bring the coconut milk to a boil, and pour it into the slow cooker. Cover and cook on the high-heat setting for 4 hours or the low-heat setting for 8 hours.

3 Finish the stew
Season the stew to taste with salt and pepper. Ladle the stew over steamed rice and serve.

Canola oil, ¼ cup (2 fl oz/ 60 ml)

Boneless beef chuck, 3 lb (1.5 kg), cut into 2-inch (5-cm) cubes

Yellow onion, 1, chopped

Unsweetened shredded or flaked dried coconut, 2 cups (8 oz/250 g)

Light brown sugar, 1 tablespoon

Ground coriander, 1 tablespoon

Ground cumin, 1½ teaspoons

Salt and freshly ground pepper

Coconut milk, 4 cups (32 fl oz/1 l)

Steamed white rice, for serving

SERVES 6–8

sauerbraten with red cabbage

Boneless beef chuck roast,
3½–4 lb (1.75–2 kg)

Salt and freshly ground pepper

Ground ginger, 1 teaspoon

Yellow onions, 2, chopped

Beef broth, 1 cup (8 fl oz/250 ml)

Cider vinegar, ¾ cup (6 fl oz/180 ml)

Dark brown sugar, ½ cup (3½ oz/105 g) firmly packed

Bay leaf, 1

Red cabbage, ½ head, halved lengthwise, cored, and thinly shredded crosswise

Gingersnap cookies, 12–16, finely crushed

SERVES 8

1 Start the sauerbraten
Season the chuck roast on all sides with salt and pepper. Sprinkle with the ground ginger and pat the seasonings into the meat. Put the roast in the slow cooker and add the onions. In a small saucepan over high heat, combine the broth and vinegar and bring to a boil. Add the brown sugar and stir until it dissolves. Pour the liquid over the roast and add the bay leaf.

2 Cook the sauerbraten
Cover and cook on the high-heat setting for 3 hours or the low-heat setting for 7 hours. Add the cabbage, using a wooden spoon to press it down into the liquid all around the roast. Sprinkle the cabbage with 1 teaspoon salt. Cover and continue cooking for 1 hour longer.

3 Finish the sauerbraten
Remove and discard the bay leaf. Transfer the roast to a cutting board, and transfer the braised cabbage to a serving bowl. Stir enough of the crushed gingersnaps into the liquid in the slow cooker to form a thick gravy. Season to taste with salt and pepper. Slice the meat across the grain. Divide the meat and braised cabbage among individual plates. Spoon the gravy on top and serve.

cook's tip

Sauerbraten is traditionally marinated for 1 or up to 2 days. To marinate the meat before cooking, boil the broth, vinegar, and brown sugar, stirring to dissolve the sugar. Let cool to room temperature. Season the roast and place in a container. Pour the vinegar mixture over the top, cover, and refrigerate for up to 2 days, turning occasionally, before proceeding with step 2.

cook's tip

For an easy mint pilaf to serve
with the curry, steam 2 cups
(14 oz/440 g) basmati rice,
following the package directions.
Just before serving, add about
3 tablespoons minced fresh
mint and fluff the mint and rice
together with a pair of forks.

indian lamb & spinach curry

1 Sauté the vegetables and spices
In a large frying pan over medium-high heat, warm the oil. Add the onions and garlic and sauté until golden, about 5 minutes. Stir in the ginger, cumin, cayenne, and turmeric and sauté until fragrant, about 30 seconds longer. Pour in the broth, raise the heat to high, and deglaze the pan, stirring to scrape up the browned bits on the pan bottom. When the broth comes to a boil, remove the pan from the heat.

2 Cook the curry
Put the lamb in the slow cooker and sprinkle with 1 tablespoon salt. Pour in the contents of the frying pan. Cover and cook on the high-heat setting for 4 hours or the low-heat setting for 8 hours.

3 Finish the curry
Add the baby spinach to the curry and cook, stirring occasionally, until the spinach is wilted, about 5 minutes. Just before serving, stir 1 1/3 cups (11 oz/345 g) of the yogurt into the curry. Season to taste with salt. Spoon the curry into shallow bowls and serve, passing the remaining yogurt at the table.

Canola oil, 1/3 cup (3 fl oz/ 80 ml)

Yellow onions, 3, chopped

Garlic, 4 cloves, minced

Ginger, 2-inch (5-cm) piece, peeled and grated

Ground cumin, 2 teaspoons

Cayenne pepper, 1 1/2 teaspoons

Ground turmeric, 1 1/2 teaspoons

Beef broth, 2 cups (16 fl oz/ 500 ml)

Boneless leg of lamb, 3 lb (1.5 kg), cut into 1-inch (2.5-cm) cubes

Salt

Baby spinach, 6 cups (6 oz/185 g)

Plain yogurt, 2 cups (1 lb/500 g)

SERVES 6–8

29

30 minutes
hands-on time

butternut squash soup

Unsalted butter,
4 tablespoons (2 oz/60 g)

Yellow onion, 1, chopped

Ginger, 2-inch (5-cm) piece,
peeled and grated

Ground cinnamon,
½ teaspoon

Ground nutmeg,
⅛ teaspoon

Butternut squash, 2,
about 4 lb (2 kg) total weight,
peeled and cut into chunks

Brown sugar, 1 tablespoon

**Salt and ground white
pepper**

Vegetable broth, 4 cups
(32 fl oz/1 l)

Sour cream, ½ cup
(4 oz/125 g)

**Fresh chives or flat-leaf
(Italian) parsley,** chopped,
for garnish

SERVES 6–8

1 Sauté the vegetables

In a frying pan over medium heat, melt the butter. Add the onion and sauté until softened, about 5 minutes. Add the ginger, cinnamon, and nutmeg and sauté until fragrant, about 1 minute longer.

2 Cook the soup

Put the squash chunks in the slow cooker and sprinkle with the brown sugar, ½ teaspoon salt, and ¼ teaspoon white pepper. Pour the contents of the frying pan over the squash and add the broth. Cover and cook on the high-heat setting for 3 hours or the low-heat setting for 6 hours.

3 Finish the soup

Using a blender or food processor, working in batches, process the squash mixture to a smooth purée. Return the soup to the slow cooker to keep warm until serving. Season to taste with salt and pepper. Ladle into bowls, garnish with a dollop of the sour cream and the chives, and serve.

cook's tip

For a vegetarian version of the soup, omit the ham hock and use vegetable broth in place of the chicken broth. To round out your menu, accompany the soup with a tossed green salad and a loaf of crusty country bread.

split pea soup with ham

1 Cook the soup

In a frying pan over medium heat, warm the oil. Add the onion and garlic and sauté until softened, 4–5 minutes. Put the ham hock in the center of the slow cooker and spread the split peas around it. Add the sautéed onion and garlic, the carrots, and the celery. Add the broth, thyme, 1 teaspoon salt, and ½ teaspoon pepper. Cover and cook on the high-heat setting for 4–5 hours or the low-heat setting for 8–10 hours, until the peas are very tender.

2 Finish the soup

Transfer the ham hock to a platter or cutting board and let cool until it can be handled, about 15 minutes. Using your fingers or a knife and fork, remove the meat from the bone, shredding or cutting the meat into bite-sized pieces. Stir the meat back into the soup along with the parsley. Ladle the soup into bowls and serve.

Olive oil, 2 tablespoons

Yellow onion, 1, finely chopped

Garlic, 2 cloves, minced

Smoked ham hock, 1, about 1½ lb (750 g)

Green split peas, 1 lb (500 g), picked over and rinsed

Carrots, 3, chopped

Celery, 2 stalks, chopped

Chicken broth, 6 cups (48 fl oz/1.5 l)

Dried thyme, 1 teaspoon

Salt and freshly ground pepper

Fresh flat-leaf (Italian) parsley, ½ cup (¾ oz/ 20 g) chopped

SERVES 6–8

chicken tagine

Flour, ¼ cup (1½ oz/45 g)

Salt and freshly ground black pepper

Bone-in, skin-on Chicken thighs, 6, about 3 lb (1.5 kg) total weight

Olive oil, ¼ cup (2 fl oz/60 ml)

Ground cumin, 2 teaspoons

Cayenne pepper, 1½ teaspoons

Chicken broth, 2 cups (16 fl oz/500 ml)

Fresh flat-leaf (Italian) parsley, ½ cup (¾ oz/20 g) coarsely chopped, plus more for garnish

Garlic, 2 cloves, crushed

Diced tomatoes, 1 can (28 oz/875 g), drained

Lemons, 3, cut into quarters

Chickpeas (garbanzo beans), 1 can (15 oz/470 g), drained and rinsed

SERVES 6

1 Brown the chicken

On a large plate, stir together the flour, 1 teaspoon salt, and ½ teaspoon black pepper. Coat the chicken thighs evenly with the flour mixture, shaking off the excess; reserve the remaining flour mixture. In a large frying pan over medium-high heat, warm the oil. Add the chicken thighs, skin side down, and cook until golden brown, 7–10 minutes. Turn the thighs over and brown for 2–3 minutes longer. Transfer the chicken thighs to the slow cooker.

2 Deglaze the pan

Pour off all but about 1 tablespoon fat from the frying pan and return the pan to medium-high heat. Add the cumin, cayenne, and the reserved flour mixture and stir briefly with a wooden spoon just until fragrant. Pour in the broth. Raise the heat to high, bring to a boil, and deglaze the pan, stirring to scrape up the browned bits on the pan bottom. Pour the contents of the pan over the chicken.

3 Cook the stew

Add the ½ cup chopped parsley, the garlic, and tomatoes to the slow cooker. Tuck 4 of the lemon quarters around the chicken thighs. Cover and cook on the high-heat setting for 1½ hours or the low-heat setting for 4 hours. Stir in the chickpeas and cook for 1 hour longer. Remove and discard the lemon quarters. Season the stew to taste with salt and black pepper. Serve, garnished with parsley and the remaining lemon quarters.

cook's tip

This Moroccan-style chicken stew is typically served on a bed of couscous, tiny beads of steamed semolina. Quick-cooking couscous is widely available in many markets; serve it plain, or mix in raisins, currants, or toasted almonds.

cook's tip

You can substitute 3 lb (1.5 kg) boneless pork shoulder, cut into 2-inch (5-cm) chunks, for the chicken. The cooking time should be increased to 3–4 hours at the high-heat setting, or 6–8 hours at the low-heat setting.

cuban chicken

1 Brown the chicken

Season the chicken pieces with salt and pepper. In a large frying pan over medium-high heat, warm the oil. Add the chicken pieces, in batches if necessary, skin side down, and cook until golden brown on the bottom, about 7 minutes. Turn the chicken and cook on the second side until lightly browned, about 3 minutes longer. Transfer to the slow cooker.

2 Deglaze the pan

Pour off all but about 1 tablespoon fat from the frying pan and return the pan to medium-high heat. Add the garlic and sauté just until fragrant, about 1 minute. Pour in the orange and lime juices. Raise the heat to high, bring to a boil, and deglaze the pan, stirring to scrape up the browned bits on the pan bottom. Pour the contents of the pan over the chicken.

3 Cook the stew

Add the bay leaf, spread the onions on top, and sprinkle with 1 teaspoon salt. Cover and cook on the high-heat setting for 2½ hours or the low-heat setting for 5 hours. Remove and discard the bay leaf. Transfer the chicken to a serving dish. Season the sauce to taste with salt and a generous amount of pepper. Spoon the onions and sauce over the chicken, garnish with the parsley, and serve, passing the lime wedges at the table.

Whole chicken, about 4 lb (2 kg), cut into 8 serving pieces

Salt and freshly ground pepper

Olive oil, 3 tablespoons

Garlic, 8 cloves, coarsely chopped

Orange juice, ¾ cup (6 fl oz/180 ml)

Lime juice, ¾ cup (6 fl oz/ 180 ml), from about 5 limes

Bay leaf, 1

Yellow onion, 1, thinly sliced

Fresh flat-leaf (Italian) parsley, ½ cup (¾ oz/ 20 g) minced

Limes, 2, cut into wedges

SERVES 6

coq
au vin

Whole chicken,
about 4 lb (2 kg), cut into
8 serving pieces

**Salt and freshly ground
pepper**

Unsalted butter,
2 tablespoons

Thick-cut bacon, 6 oz
(185 g), chopped

Button mushrooms,
¾ lb (375 g) halved

Yellow onions, 2, finely
chopped

Garlic, 3 cloves,
thinly sliced

Carrots, 2, finely chopped

Flour, 3 tablespoons

Dry red wine, 1 bottle
(24 fl oz/750 ml)

Chicken broth, 2 cups
(16 fl oz/500 ml)

Fresh thyme, 3 sprigs

Cooked egg noodles,
for serving

SERVES 6

1 **Brown the chicken**
Season the chicken pieces with salt and pepper.
In a large frying pan over medium heat, melt the butter. Add
the bacon and cook, stirring, until browned, about 5 minutes.
Transfer the bacon to paper towels to drain. Add the chicken
pieces, in batches if necessary, skin side down, and cook until
golden brown on the bottom, 8–10 minutes. (You don't need
to turn them.) Transfer the chicken pieces to the slow cooker
and scatter the bacon on top.

2 **Sauté the vegetables**
Pour off all but 2–3 tablespoons fat from the frying pan
and return the pan to high heat. Add the mushrooms and sauté
until golden, 4–5 minutes. Add the onions, garlic, and carrots,
and sauté until the onions are softened, about 2 minutes longer.
Sprinkle with the flour and sauté, stirring, for about 1 minute
longer. Pour in the wine, bring to a boil, and deglaze the pan,
stirring to scrape up the browned bits on the pan bottom. Pour
in the broth and return the liquid to a boil. Pour the contents
of the pan over the chicken.

3 **Cook the chicken**
Tuck the thyme sprigs around the chicken pieces. Cover
and cook on the high-heat setting for 2½ hours or the low-heat
setting for 5 hours. Remove and discard the thyme sprigs.
Season to taste with salt and pepper. Spoon over the cooked
egg noodles and serve.

cook's tip

Use a medium- or full-bodied red wine for cooking the chicken, and then drink the same wine with the meal. Or, try using a dry white wine in place of the red wine for a lighter but equally delicious dish.

chicken & sausage gumbo

1 Cook the chicken

In a large frying pan over medium-high heat, warm 1 tablespoon of the oil. Add the chicken and cook, stirring occasionally, until lightly browned on all sides, about 8 minutes. Transfer the chicken to the slow cooker, then add the sausages. Scatter the okra, bell pepper, celery, and onion on top.

2 Make the roux

Return the frying pan to medium heat and add the remaining 1 tablespoon oil. Sprinkle the flour in the pan and cook, stirring constantly, until golden brown, about 4 minutes. Stir in the broth and the tomatoes with their juice and raise the heat to medium-high. When the mixture comes to a boil, remove the pan from the heat. Season with ½ teaspoon salt and the cayenne and then pour over the vegetables, chicken, and sausages.

3 Cook the gumbo

Cover and cook on the high-heat setting for 4 hours or the low-heat setting for 8 hours. Season to taste with salt and cayenne. Ladle the gumbo over steamed rice and serve.

Olive oil, 2 tablespoons

Skinless, boneless chicken thighs, 4, cut into 1½-inch (4-cm) pieces

Andouille or other spicy smoked sausages, ¾ lb (375 g), cut into 1-inch (2.5-cm) slices

Okra, ½ lb (250 g), cut crosswise into thick slices

Red or green bell pepper (capsicum), 1, seeded and chopped

Celery, 3 stalks, chopped

Yellow onion, 1, chopped

Flour, 2 tablespoons

Chicken broth, 2 cups (16 fl oz/500 ml)

Diced plum (Roma) tomatoes, 1 can (14½ oz/455 g), with juice

Salt

Cayenne pepper, ¼ teaspoon

Steamed white rice, for serving

SERVES 4–6

43

braised moroccan lamb chops

Flour, ¼ cup (1½ oz/45 g)

Salt and freshly ground pepper

Lamb shoulder chops,
4 lb (2 kg) total weight, each about 1 inch (2.5 cm) thick, trimmed of excess fat

Olive oil, 3 tablespoons

Yellow onion, 1, finely chopped

Ground cumin, 1 teaspoon

Paprika, 1 teaspoon

Beef broth, 2 cups
(16 fl oz/500 ml)

Lemon juice, from
1 lemon

Green olives, 1½ cups
(7½ oz/235 g), well drained, pitted if desired

Fresh mint, ½ cup (¾ oz/
20 g) minced

SERVES 6–8

1 Brown the lamb

On a large plate, stir together the flour and 1 teaspoon salt. Coat the lamb chops evenly with the flour mixture, shaking off the excess; reserve the remaining flour mixture. In a large frying pan over medium-high heat, warm the oil. Add the lamb chops, in batches if necessary, and cook, turning once, until browned, about 3 minutes on each side. Transfer the chops to the slow cooker.

2 Make the sauce

Pour off all but about 1 tablespoon fat from the frying pan and return the pan to medium-high heat. Add the onion and sauté until translucent, 2–3 minutes. Sprinkle with the cumin, paprika, and reserved flour mixture and sauté briefly, just until fragrant. Pour in the broth and lemon juice. Raise the heat to high, bring to a boil, and deglaze the pan, stirring to scrape up the browned bits on the pan bottom. Pour the contents of the pan over the lamb.

3 Braise the lamb

Cover and cook on the high-heat setting for 3–4 hours or the low-heat setting for 6–8 hours. The lamb should be very tender. About 1 hour before the lamb is ready, add the olives. When the lamb is ready, transfer it to a platter and cover with aluminum foil to keep warm. Skim off any excess fat from the surface of the sauce. Season the sauce to taste with salt and pepper. Stir in the mint. Leave the chops on the platter or transfer to individual plates. Spoon the sauce with the olives and mint over the lamb and serve.

cook's tip

For a complete meal, serve the
fragrantly seasoned braised lamb
over freshly steamed couscous,
mashed potatoes, or steamed
rice to soak up all the juices.

cook's tip

Other dried fruit, such as pears,
apples, cherries, or figs, can also
be used in this dish. Use one or
a combination of fruits to equal
a total of 3 cups (18 oz/560 g).

pork roast with dried-fruit compote

1 Brown the pork

Season the pork shoulder on all sides with salt and pepper. In a large frying pan over medium-high heat, warm the oil. Add the pork and brown well on all sides, about 10 minutes total. Transfer the pork to the slow cooker. Pour off the excess fat from the frying pan and return the pan to high heat. Pour in the broth, wine, and orange juice and deglaze the pan, stirring to scrape up the browned bits on the pan bottom. Stir in the brown sugar, bring the liquid to a boil, and pour the contents of the pan over the pork.

2 Cook the pork

Add the rosemary sprig to the slow cooker. Scatter the plums and apricots around the sides of the meat. Cover and cook on the high-heat setting for 4 hours or the low-heat setting for 8 hours.

3 Carve the pork

Remove and discard the rosemary sprig. Transfer the pork to a platter and spoon the fruit compote around the pork. Slice the pork across the grain, or, if the meat is too tender to slice neatly, use a pair of forks to tear it into large chunks. Serve with the compote alongside.

Bone-in pork shoulder, about 3 lb (1.5 kg)

Salt and freshly ground pepper

Olive oil, 3 tablespoons

Chicken broth, 1 cup (8 fl oz/250 ml)

Dry white wine, 3/4 cup (6 fl oz/180 ml)

Orange juice, 1/2 cup (4 fl oz/125 ml)

Dark brown sugar, 1/4 cup (2 oz/60 g) firmly packed

Fresh rosemary, 1 sprig

Dried plums, 1 1/2 cups (9 oz/280 g), pitted

Dried apricots, 1 1/2 cups (9 oz/280 g)

SERVES 8

pork loin
with apples & sage

Boneless pork loin,
2½–3 lb (1.25–1.5 kg), trimmed of excess fat, rolled, and tied

Salt and freshly ground pepper

Canola oil, 2 tablespoons

Dried sage, 2 teaspoons

Yellow onion, ½, chopped

Garlic, 2 cloves, minced

Chicken broth, 1 cup (8 fl oz/250 ml)

Apple cider or unsweetened apple juice, 1 cup (8 fl oz/250 ml)

Cinnamon stick, 1 small

Granny Smith apples, 6, halved, cored, and cut into wedges

Cornstarch (cornflour), 2 tablespoons

SERVES 6–8

1 Brown the pork
Season the pork loin on all sides with salt and pepper. In a large frying pan over medium-high heat, warm the oil. Add the pork and brown well on all sides, about 10 minutes total. Transfer to the slow cooker. Sprinkle the sage over the roast.

2 Make the sauce
Return the frying pan to medium-high heat. Add the onion and garlic and sauté until softened, 2–3 minutes. Add the broth and ½ cup (4 fl oz/125 ml) of the cider, bring to a boil, and deglaze the pan, stirring to scrape up the browned bits on the pan bottom. Pour over the pork. Add the cinnamon stick, cover, and cook on the high-heat setting for 2–3 hours or the low-heat setting for 5–6 hours. Arrange the apple slices around the meat, cover, and continue cooking for 1 hour longer, until the apples are tender.

3 Finish the sauce
Transfer the pork to a cutting board and remove the strings. Transfer the apple slices to a bowl. Cover the pork and the apples with aluminum foil to keep warm. Put the slow cooker on the high-heat setting. In a small bowl, stir the cornstarch into the remaining ½ cup cider until dissolved. Slowly pour the cider-cornstarch mixture into the cooking liquid in the slow cooker while stirring constantly. Continue stirring until it thickens to a creamy consistency, 3–5 minutes. Season to taste with salt and pepper. Slice the pork across the grain and serve with the apples. Spoon the gravy on top.

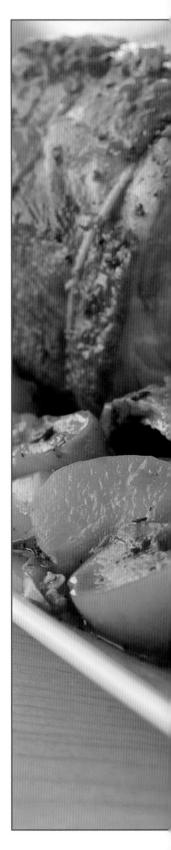

cook's tip

To save time in the kitchen,
ask the butcher to tie the roast
for you, or purchase it already
tied. The compact shape ensures
even cooking and neat slices.

cook's tip

Serve these hearty sandwiches
with homemade or good-quality
prepared coleslaw or potato
salad from your favorite deli
or upscale market. Traditionally,
coleslaw is served atop the pork
in the sandwich.

pulled pork

1 Brown the pork

In a large frying pan over medium-high heat, warm the oil. Add the pork pieces and brown well on all sides, about 12 minutes total. Transfer the pork to the slow cooker.

2 Make the sauce and cook the pork

Pour off all but about 1 tablespoon fat from the frying pan and return the pan to medium-high heat. Add the onion and sauté until golden, about 5 minutes. Add the vinegar and deglaze the pan, stirring to scrape up the browned bits on the pan bottom. Stir in the ketchup, brown sugar, molasses, red pepper flakes, Worcestershire sauce, mustard, and 1 teaspoon each salt and pepper. Cook, stirring occasionally, just until the mixture begins to bubble. Pour over the pork. Cover and cook on the high-heat setting for 4–5 hours or the low-heat setting for 8–10 hours. The pork should be very tender.

3 Shred the pork and serve

Transfer the pork pieces to a platter. Using a pair of forks, shred each piece of pork, removing and discarding any large pieces of fat. Skim off the excess fat from the surface of the sauce and return the pulled pork to the sauce. Stir together to combine. Serve the pork and sauce atop the sandwich rolls.

Canola or corn oil, 3 tablespoons

Boneless pork shoulder, 4 lb (2 kg), cut into 3 equal pieces

Yellow onion, 1, finely chopped

Cider vinegar, 3/4 cup (6 fl oz/180 ml)

Tomato ketchup, 3/4 cup (6 oz/185 g)

Brown sugar, 1/3 cup (2 1/2 oz/75 g) firmly packed

Light molasses, 1/4 cup (2 3/4 oz/80 g)

Red pepper flakes, 2 teaspoons

Worcestershire sauce, 1 tablespoon

Dry mustard, 1 teaspoon

Salt and freshly ground pepper

Soft sandwich rolls, split and toasted, for serving

SERVES 6–8

beef-chipotle chili

Flour, ¼ cup (1½ oz/45 g)

Salt and freshly ground pepper

Boneless beef chuck,
3 lb (1.5 kg), trimmed of excess fat and cut into chunks

Olive oil, 4–6 tablespoons (2–3 fl oz/60–90 ml)

Dried oregano,
1½ teaspoons

Garlic, 4 cloves, minced

Red onions, 2, finely chopped

Beef broth, 2 cups (16 fl oz/500 ml)

Chipotle chiles in adobo sauce, 1 can (7 oz/220 g)

SERVES 6–8

1 Brown the beef

In a resealable plastic bag, combine the flour, 1 teaspoon salt, and ½ teaspoon pepper. Add the beef chunks and shake to coat evenly with the flour mixture; reserve the excess flour mixture. In a large frying pan over medium-high heat, warm 4 tablespoons (2 fl oz/60 ml) of the oil. Add half of the beef chunks and cook, turning as needed, until evenly browned on all sides, 10–12 minutes. Transfer to paper towels to drain briefly, and then transfer to the slow cooker. Repeat with the remaining beef chunks, adding the remaining 2 tablespoons oil if needed. Sprinkle the oregano over the meat.

2 Sauté the vegetables

Return the pan to medium-high heat. Add the garlic and all but about ½ cup (2½ oz/75 g) of the onions and sauté until fragrant, about 1 minute. Sprinkle with the reserved flour mixture and sauté for about 1 minute longer. Pour in the broth and add the chipotle chiles with their sauce, breaking up the chiles coarsely with your fingers. Raise the heat to high, bring to a boil, and deglaze the pan, stirring to scrape up the browned bits on the pan bottom. Pour over the beef.

3 Cook the chili

Cover and cook on the high-heat setting for 3–4 hours or the low-heat setting for 6–8 hours. The beef should be very tender. Spoon the chili into bowls, sprinkle with the remaining ½ cup chopped onion, and serve.

cook's tip

Substitute a dark Mexican beer
for all or part of the beef broth.
It will give the chili a rich, earthy
flavor. Bottles of the same
chilled beer would also make
an excellent accompaniment
to this spicy, smoky chili.

cook's tip

Serve the barbecue brisket alongside homemade or good-quality purchased potato salad or mashed potatoes. Leftover brisket is perfect piled high on large seeded buns.

barbecue-style brisket

1 Brown the brisket

On a large plate, stir together the flour, 1 teaspoon salt, and ½ teaspoon black pepper. Coat the brisket evenly with the flour mixture, shaking off the excess; reserve the remaining flour mixture. In a large frying pan over high heat, warm the oil. Add the brisket, fattier side down, and cook until browned on the bottom, about 7 minutes. Turn the brisket over and brown the second side, about 7 minutes longer. Transfer the brisket, fat side up, to the slow cooker.

2 Sauté the vegetables

Pour off all but about 1 tablespoon fat from the frying pan and return the pan to medium-high heat. Add the onions, garlic, and cayenne and sauté until the onions begin to turn translucent, 2–3 minutes. Stir in the reserved flour mixture and cook for 1 minute longer. Pour in the broth and vinegar. Raise the heat to high, bring to a boil, and deglaze the pan, stirring to scrape up the browned bits on the pan bottom. Add the sugar and tomato paste and stir until evenly blended. Pour over the brisket.

3 Cook the brisket

Cover and cook on the high-heat setting for 3–4 hours or the low-heat setting for 6–8 hours. The meat should be very tender when pierced with a fork. Transfer the brisket to a cutting board. Cover with aluminum foil and let rest for 10 minutes. Meanwhile, skim off the excess fat from the surface of the sauce. Slice the meat across the grain. Spoon the sauce over the meat and serve.

Flour, ¼ cup (1½ oz/45 g)

Salt and freshly ground black pepper

Beef brisket, 3½–4 lb (1.75–2 kg), trimmed of excess fat

Olive oil, ¼ cup (2 fl oz/ 60 ml)

Yellow onions, 2, thinly sliced

Garlic, 2 cloves, minced

Cayenne pepper, 1 teaspoon

Beef broth, 1 cup (8 fl oz/ 250 ml)

Red wine vinegar, ½ cup (4 fl oz/125 ml)

Sugar, ⅓ cup (3 oz/90 g)

Tomato paste, 2 tablespoons

SERVES 6–8

italian
pot roast

Flour, ¼ cup (1½ oz/45 g)

Salt and freshly ground pepper

Boneless beef chuck, 4 lb (2 kg), trimmed of excess fat and tied

Olive oil, ¼ cup (2 fl oz/60 ml)

Garlic, 4 cloves, minced

Dry red wine, 1 cup (8 fl oz/250 ml)

Whole plum (Roma) tomatoes, 1 can (28 oz/ 875 g), drained

Dried oregano, 1 tablespoon

Sugar, 2 teaspoons

Bay leaves, 2

Fresh basil, ¼ cup (⅓ oz/ 10 g) slivered

SERVES 6–8

1 Brown the pot roast

On a large plate, stir together the flour, 1 teaspoon salt, and ½ teaspoon pepper. Coat the beef evenly with the flour mixture, shaking off the excess; reserve the remaining flour mixture. In a large frying pan over high heat, warm the oil. Add the roast and brown it well on all sides, 12–15 minutes total. Transfer the roast to the slow cooker.

2 Deglaze the pan

Pour off all but about 1 tablespoon fat from the frying pan and return the pan to medium-high heat. Add the garlic and sauté for a few seconds until fragrant. Sprinkle with the reserved flour mixture and cook, stirring, about 1 minute longer. Pour in the red wine and deglaze the pan, stirring to scrape up the browned bits on the pan bottom. Pour over the roast.

3 Cook the pot roast

Using your hands, break up the tomatoes as you add them to the slow cooker. Add the oregano, sugar, and bay leaves. Cover and cook on the high-heat setting for 3–4 hours or the low-heat setting for 6–8 hours. The meat should be very tender when pierced with a fork. Remove and discard the bay leaves. Transfer the roast to a cutting board and remove the strings. Cover with aluminum foil and let rest for about 10 minutes. Meanwhile, skim off and discard the excess fat from the surface of the sauce. Stir in the basil. Slice the roast across the grain and arrange the slices on a platter or individual plates. Spoon the sauce over the meat and serve.

cook's tip

For an easy side dish, cook
orzo or another small pasta
until al dente, according to the
package directions, and toss
it with a little butter and freshly
grated Parmesan cheese.

cook's tip

To make the classic osso buco garnish known as *gremolata*, combine 1 tablespoon each chopped fresh flat-leaf (Italian) parsley and grated lemon zest, and 1 clove garlic, finely minced. Scatter the *gremolata* over each serving. Osso buco is traditionally served with saffron risotto, but steamed rice or quick polenta are also excellent accompaniments.

osso buco with mushrooms & peas

1 Brown the veal

On a large plate, stir together the flour, 1 teaspoon salt, and ½ teaspoon pepper. Coat the veal shanks evenly with the flour mixture, shaking off the excess; reserve the remaining flour mixture. In a large frying pan over medium-high heat, warm the oil. Add the veal shanks and cook, turning once, until browned on both sides, about 5 minutes on each side. Transfer to the slow cooker and scatter the mushrooms on top.

2 Sauté the shallots

Return the frying pan to medium-high heat, add the shallots, and sauté until tender and beginning to brown, about 3 minutes. Sprinkle with the reserved flour mixture and sauté for about 1 minute longer. Pour in the broth and deglaze the pan, stirring to scrape up the browned bits on the pan bottom. Pour over the veal.

3 Cook the veal

Tuck the thyme sprigs around the veal shanks. Cover and cook on the high-heat setting for 2 hours or the low-heat setting for 4½ hours. Scatter the peas on top, gently immerse them in the hot liquid with a large spoon, and continue to cook for 30 minutes longer. Remove and discard the thyme sprigs. Transfer the veal pieces to 6 plates, taking care that they don't fall apart. Season the sauce to taste with salt and pepper. Spoon the sauce, mushrooms, and peas over the veal and serve.

Flour, ¼ cup (1½ oz/45 g)

Salt and freshly ground pepper

Veal shanks, 6, about 3 lb (1.5 kg) total weight, each cut for osso buco into slices about 1 inch (2.5 cm) thick

Olive oil, ¼ cup (2 fl oz/ 60 ml)

Fresh cremini or shiitake mushrooms, 1½ cups (45 g), halved if large

Shallots, 4 large, chopped

Beef broth, 2 cups (16 fl oz/500 ml)

Fresh thyme, 2 sprigs

Frozen peas, 2 cups (8 oz/250 g)

SERVES 6

beef stew
with bacon

Thick-cut bacon, 4 oz (125 g), chopped

Flour, 3 tablespoons

Salt and freshly ground pepper

Boneless beef chuck, 3 lb (1.5 kg), trimmed of excess fat and cut into chunks

Fresh cremini mushrooms, ¾ lb (375 g), halved if large

Baby carrots, ½ lb (250 g)

Frozen pearl onions, ½ lb (250 g)

Garlic, 3 cloves, minced

Dry red wine, 1 cup (8 fl oz/ 250 ml)

Beef broth, 1 cup (8 fl oz/ 250 ml)

Tomato paste, 2 tablespoons

Fresh rosemary, 1 tablespoon minced

SERVES 6

1 Cook the bacon
In a large frying pan over medium heat, cook the bacon, stirring occasionally, until crisp, 5–7 minutes. Transfer the bacon to paper towels to drain. Pour off the drippings into a small heatproof bowl, leaving about 1 tablespoon drippings in the pan. Set the pan, reserved drippings, and bacon aside.

2 Brown the beef
In a resealable plastic bag, combine the flour, 1 teaspoon salt, and ½ teaspoon pepper. Add the beef chunks and shake to coat evenly with the flour mixture. Return the frying pan to medium-high heat. When the drippings are hot, add half of the beef chunks and cook, turning once, until well browned, about 5 minutes on each side. Transfer the beef to the slow cooker. Repeat with the remaining beef chunks, adding the reserved drippings if needed. Scatter the mushrooms, carrots, onions, and garlic on top.

3 Cook the stew
Return the pan to medium-high heat and add the wine, broth, and tomato paste. Mix well, bring to a boil, and deglaze the pan, stirring to scrape up the browned bits on the pan bottom. Pour the contents of the pan over the vegetables and beef. Cover and cook on the high-heat setting for 4–5 hours or the low-heat setting for 8–9 hours. The beef should be very tender. Stir in the reserved bacon and the rosemary. Cook, uncovered, on the high-heat setting for 10 minutes longer to thicken the sauce slightly. Season to taste with salt and pepper and serve.

cook's tip

Using frozen pearl onions saves time and labor, but if you prefer, substitute 1 large yellow onion, chopped, for the pearl onions.

ale-braised
short ribs

1 Brown the short ribs

Preheat the broiler (grill). Generously season the ribs on all sides with salt and pepper. Working in batches if necessary, arrange the ribs on a broiler pan and place under the broiler. Broil (grill) the ribs, turning once, until well browned, about 3 minutes on each side. Transfer the ribs to the slow cooker.

2 Cook the short ribs

Scatter the onions and garlic over the ribs. Add the squash. Pour in the tomatoes with their juice and the ale. Cover and cook on the high-heat setting for 5–6 hours or the low-heat setting for 7–8 hours. The meat should be separating from the bones and the squash should be tender.

3 Thicken the sauce

Using a slotted spoon, transfer the ribs and squash to a shallow bowl or platter and cover loosely with aluminum foil to keep warm. Skim off the excess fat from the surface of the sauce. Put the slow cooker on the high-heat setting. In a small bowl, whisk together the flour and ¼ cup (2 fl oz/60 ml) water. Whisk the flour mixture into the sauce and cook, uncovered and stirring occasionally, until the sauce is slightly thickened, about 15 minutes. Season to taste with salt and pepper. Spoon the sauce over the ribs and squash and serve.

Bone-in beef short ribs, 4–5 lb (2–2.5 kg), cut into 3-inch (7.5-cm) pieces

Salt and freshly ground pepper

Yellow onions, 2, thinly sliced

Garlic, 3 cloves, sliced

Butternut squash, 1, about 2 lb (1 kg) total weight, peeled and cut into chunks

Diced plum (Roma) tomatoes, 1 can (14½ oz/ 455 g), with juice

Ale or dark beer, 1 bottle (12 fl oz/375 ml)

Flour, 3 tablespoons

SERVES 6

make more
to store

penne with ratatouille

RATATOUILLE

Olive oil, ¼ cup (2 fl oz/ 60 ml)

Yellow onions, 4, chopped

Garlic, 4 cloves, chopped

Plum (Roma) tomatoes, 10, halved, seeded, and cut into chunks

Zucchini (courgettes), 6 medium, cut into chunks

Eggplants (aubergines), 2 medium, trimmed and cut into chunks

Red bell peppers (capsicums), 3 large, seeded and cut into chunks

Vegetable broth, ½ cup (4 fl oz/120 ml)

Fresh thyme and fresh oregano, 1 teaspoon *each* minced

Salt and ground pepper

Penne, 1 lb (500 g)

SERVES 4

Makes about 12 cups (4½ lb/2.25 kg) ratatouille total

The flavors of this rustic Provençal stew mingle perfectly in the gentle heat of a slow cooker. This recipe yields enough for dinner tonight plus the dishes on the following pages.

1 Make the ratatouille

In a large frying pan over medium heat, warm the oil. Add the onions and garlic and sauté until tender but not brown, about 10 minutes. Transfer to the slow cooker. Add the tomatoes, zucchini, eggplants, bell peppers, broth, thyme, oregano, and 2 teaspoons each salt and pepper to the slow cooker. Stir to combine. Cover and cook on the high-heat setting for 4 hours or the low-heat setting for 8 hours. Set aside 2 cups (12 oz/375 g) of the ratatouille, and store the rest for later use (see Storage Tip, right).

2 Cook the pasta

Bring a large pot of water to a boil. Add 2 tablespoons salt and the pasta. Cook, stirring occasionally to prevent sticking, until al dente, according to the package directions. Drain the pasta, return it to the pot, and toss with the 2 cups of ratatouille. Season to taste with salt and pepper and serve.

storage tip

Let the remaining ratatouille cool
to room temperature. Store in
airtight containers or heavy-duty
resealable plastic bags in the
refrigerator for up to 2 days or in
the freezer for up to 2 months.

cook's tip

The ratatouille is also delicious served with broiled or grilled lamb chops that you've rubbed with garlic and olive oil and sprinkled with salt and pepper.

sausages
with ratatouille

1 Cook the sausages
Slit each sausage diagonally several times on each side. In a frying pan over medium heat, warm the oil. Add the sausages and cook, turning once, until browned on both sides, 8–12 minutes total.

2 Warm the ratatouille
While the sausages are cooking, put the ratatouille in a saucepan over medium heat and warm, stirring occasionally to prevent scorching, until hot, 8–10 minutes. Divide the ratatouille and sausages among 4 plates and serve.

Ratatouille (page 66), 4 cups (1.5 lb/750 g)

Smoked sausages such as kielbasa, 4 large or 8 small

Olive oil, 1 tablespoon

SERVES 4

spicy halibut with ratatouille

Ratatouille (page 66),
4 cups (1.5 lb/750 g)

Halibut fillets, 4, each about
6 oz (185 g)

Hot paprika, ¾ teaspoon

**Salt and freshly ground
pepper**

Olive oil, ¼ cup (2 fl oz/
60 ml)

SERVES 4

1 **Sauté the fish**
Season the halibut fillets on both sides with the paprika, salt, and pepper. In a large frying pan over medium-high heat, warm the oil. Add the fillets and cook, turning once, until golden brown, about 4 minutes on each side.

2 **Add the ratatouille**
Spoon the ratatouille around the halibut fillets in the pan. Cover, reduce the heat to medium, and cook, stirring the ratatouille once or twice to prevent scorching and to heat evenly, until the ratatouille is heated through and the fish fillets are opaque throughout, about 4 minutes longer. Divide the halibut and ratatouille among 4 plates and serve.

cook's tip

You can substitute other mild-flavored, firm-fleshed white fish, such as cod, tilapia, or sea bass, for the halibut.

seared tuna with white beans

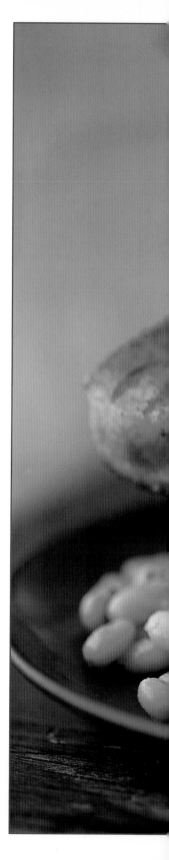

WHITE BEANS

Dried small white beans, such as cannellini or navy, 2 lb (1 kg), picked over and rinsed

Olive oil, 2 tablespoons

Yellow onion, 1, chopped

Garlic, 4 cloves

Salt and freshly ground pepper

Tuna steaks, 4, each about 4 oz (125 g) and ¾ inch (2 cm) thick

Olive oil, 3 tablespoons

Fresh flat-leaf (Italian) parsley, 2 tablespoons minced

SERVES 4

Makes about 10 cups (4 lb/2 kg) beans total

A slow cooker is ideal for cooking beans, which require many hours of gentle simmering. This recipe yields enough for this meal as well as for two of the recipes on the following pages.

1 Parboil the beans
Put the beans in a large pot and add cold water to cover. Bring to a boil over high heat, about 15 minutes. Drain the beans and transfer them to the slow cooker.

2 Cook the beans
Meanwhile, in a frying pan over medium-high heat, warm the 2 tablespoons oil. Add the onion and garlic and sauté until the onion is translucent, about 4 minutes. Add the onion, garlic, and 1½ tablespoons salt to the slow cooker and stir to combine with the beans. Add cold water to cover the beans by about 2 inches (5 cm). Cover and cook until the beans are tender, on the high-heat setting for 4 hours or the low-heat setting for 8 hours. Season to taste with salt and pepper.

3 Sear the tuna
Season the tuna steaks on both sides with salt and pepper. In a frying pan over medium-high heat, warm the 3 tablespoons oil. Add the tuna steaks and sear until crisp and browned on the outside, about 2 minutes on each side for rare. Transfer 2 cups (14 oz/440 g) of the beans to a large bowl and toss with the parsley. Store the rest of the beans for later use (see Storage Tip, right). Divide the beans among 4 plates, top each with a tuna steak, and serve.

storage tip

Let the remaining beans cool
to room temperature. Store in
airtight containers or heavy-duty
resealable plastic bags in the
refrigerator for up to 3 days or
in the freezer for up to 1 month.

cook's tip

For a creamy variation of this soup, put the beans, plus 4 cups (32 fl oz/1 l) chicken stock, 1 cup (8 fl oz/250 ml) heavy (double) cream, and the thyme in a food processor or blender and process to a smooth purée. Pour into a saucepan and warm gently over medium heat until just beginning to simmer. Do not let boil. Season to taste with salt and pepper.

white bean soup

1 Make the soup

Put 2 cups (14 oz/440 g) of the beans in a food processor or blender and purée until smooth. In a saucepan over medium heat, combine the puréed beans, the remaining 2 cups whole beans, thyme, and broth. Bring to a simmer then lower the heat to medium-low. Cook, stirring occasionally, until the flavors have blended, about 10 minutes. Season to taste with salt and pepper. Ladle the soup into bowls, drizzle each serving with olive oil, and serve.

White Beans (page 72), 4 cups (1¾ lb/875 g)

Fresh thyme, 1 teaspoon minced

Chicken broth, 6 cups (48 fl oz/1.5 l)

Salt and freshly ground pepper

Olive oil, for drizzling

SERVES 4

quick cassoulet

White Beans (page 72),
4 cups (1¾ lb/875 g)

Pork sausages, 1½ lb
(750 g)

Olive oil, 2 tablespoons

Thick-cut bacon, 5 slices,
chopped

Fresh thyme, 1 sprig

**Diced plum (Roma)
tomatoes,** 1 can
(14½ oz/455 g)

Sugar, 1½ teaspoons

**Salt and freshly ground
pepper**

Fresh bread crumbs,
1 cup (2 oz/60 g)

Unsalted butter,
4 tablespoons (2 oz/60 g),
melted

SERVES 4–6

1 Cook the sausages
Slit each sausage diagonally several times on each side. In a frying pan over medium heat, warm 1 tablespoon of the oil. Add the sausages and cook, turning once, until browned on the outside and cooked through, about 10 minutes total. Set aside.

2 Prepare the beans
In a separate large frying pan over medium heat, warm the remaining 1 tablespoon oil. Add the bacon and sauté until it starts to brown, 5–7 minutes. Drain off all but 2 tablespoons of the bacon fat. Stir in the beans, thyme, tomatoes, and sugar. Bring to a simmer and cook, stirring frequently, until the beans are heated through, about 5 minutes. Season to taste with salt and pepper.

3 Bake the cassoulet
Cut the sausages crosswise into bite-sized pieces. Butter a 3-qt (3-l) ovenproof pan or gratin dish and distribute the sausages evenly in the pan. Spoon the bean mixture over the sausages, removing and discarding the thyme sprig. Spread the bread crumbs evenly on top and drizzle with the melted butter. Bake until the beans are bubbly and the crumb topping is golden brown, about 20 minutes. Transfer to a rack to let cool slightly and serve.

cook's tip

You can substitute bite-sized pieces of other freshly cooked or leftover meats or poultry—such as leftover rotisserie chicken, roast beef or lamb, or grilled steak—for the sausages. Heat them in the frying pan along with the beans in step 2.

cook's tip

For extra flavor, stir 2 minced cloves garlic and 2 tablespoons olive oil together with 1 teaspoon each salt and pepper. Rub the mixture all over the meat. Place the meat in an airtight container and refrigerate for at least 2 hours or for up to overnight. Bring to room temperature before grilling.

grilled flank steak with white beans

1 Cook the steak

Prepare a gas or charcoal grill for direct-heat grilling over high heat and oil the grill rack. Or, preheat a broiler (grill). Season the steak on both sides with salt and pepper. Place the steak on the grill rack or put it on a broiler pan and place under the broiler. Cook, turning once, for 5–7 minutes on each side for medium-rare, or until done to your liking.

2 Warm the beans

While the steak is cooking, in a saucepan over medium heat, warm the beans, stirring frequently, until heated through, about 2 minutes.

3 Finish the dish

When the steak is ready, transfer it to a cutting board, cover loosely with aluminum foil, and let it rest for about 5 minutes. Spoon one-fourth of the hot beans onto each plate, and sprinkle with the chives. Slice the steak across the grain. Arrange some of the slices on top of each mound of beans, top with the arugula, and drizzle with olive oil. Using a vegetable peeler, cut thin shavings of Parmesan cheese onto each serving. Garnish with the lemon wedges and serve.

White Beans (page 72), 4 cups (1¾ lb/875 g)

Flank steak, 2 lb (1 kg), trimmed of excess fat

Salt and freshly ground pepper

Fresh chives or parsley, ⅓ cup (½ oz/15 g) minced

Baby arugula, 2 cups (2 oz/60 g)

Olive oil, for drizzling

Parmesan cheese, ¼-lb (125-g) wedge

Lemon, 1, cut into wedges

SERVES 4

fettuccine bolognese

BOLOGNESE SAUCE

Olive oil, 2 tablespoons

Pancetta, 2 oz (60 g), chopped

Yellow onions, 2 small, finely chopped

Carrots, 2, finely chopped

Celery, 1 stalk, finely chopped

Ground (minced) beef, 3 lb (1.5 kg)

Beef broth, 2 cups (16 fl oz/ 500 ml)

Dry red wine, 1 ½ cups (12 fl oz/375 ml)

Crushed plum (Roma) tomatoes, 1 can (28 oz/ 875 g)

Milk, ½ cup (4 fl oz/125 ml)

Salt and freshly ground pepper

Fettuccine, 1 lb (500 g)

Parmesan cheese, ½ cup (2 oz/60 g) freshly grated

SERVES 4

makes about 12 cups (3 qt/3 l) sauce total

A robust ragù gains in flavor by spending hours simmering in a slow cooker. This recipe yields a big batch so you can eat it for dinner tonight, and freeze the rest for additional dishes.

1 Sauté the ingredients
In a large frying pan over medium-high heat, warm the oil. Add the pancetta and sauté until it begins to render its fat, about 1 minute. Add the onions, carrots, and celery and sauté until the onions are translucent, about 5 minutes. Add the beef and cook, breaking up the meat with a wooden spoon, until it is no longer red, about 7 minutes. Transfer to the slow cooker. Add the broth and wine to the pan and raise the heat to high. Bring to a boil and deglaze the pan, stirring to scrape up the browned bits on the pan bottom. Pour the liquid into the slow cooker along with the tomatoes and stir to combine.

2 Cook the sauce
Cover and cook the sauce on the high-heat setting for 4 hours or the low-heat setting for 8 hours. Add the milk, stirring to combine. Cover and continue cooking for 20 minutes longer. Season to taste with salt and pepper.

3 Cook the pasta
Bring a large pot of water to a boil. Add 2 tablespoons salt and the pasta. Cook, stirring occasionally to prevent sticking, until al dente, according to the package directions. Drain, return the pasta to the pot, and toss gently with 2 cups (16 fl oz/ 500 ml) of the sauce. Serve, passing the Parmesan at the table.

storage tip

Let the remaining Bolognese
sauce cool to room temperature.
Store in airtight containers in the
refrigerator for up to 3 days or
in the freezer for up to 3 months.

cook's tip

If using instant or regular polenta instead of the prepared tube, cook the polenta according to the package directions, spread onto a rimmed baking sheet, and let cool. Use a biscuit cutter or an inverted glass to cut it into rounds before proceeding.

polenta gratin
with bolognese

1 **Prepare the gratin**
Preheat the oven to 400°F (200°C). Butter a gratin dish or a 10-by-12-inch (25-by-30-cm) baking dish. Remove the polenta from its plastic tube and cut the cylinder crosswise into slices about ¼ inch (6 mm) thick. Arrange the slices, overlapping them, in the prepared dish. Spoon the sauce around the polenta and sprinkle the Parmesan over the sauce.

2 **Bake the gratin**
Bake until the sauce is hot and bubbly, about 20 minutes. Serve garnished with the parsley.

**Bolognese Sauce
(page 80),** 4 cups
(32 fl oz/1 l)

Unsalted butter, for greasing

Prepared polenta tube,
1½ lb (750 g)

Parmesan cheese, ½ cup
(2 oz/60 g) freshly grated

**Fresh flat-leaf (Italian)
parsley or basil,**
3 tablespoons minced

SERVES 4

roasted eggplant lasagna

**Bolognese Sauce
(page 80),** 3 cups (24 fl oz/
750 ml)

Eggplants (aubergines),
2, about 1½ lb (750 g) total
weight, cut crosswise into
slices ½ inch (12 mm) thick

Olive oil, for brushing

**Salt and freshly ground
pepper**

Fresh mozzarella cheese,
1 lb (500 g), sliced

Parmesan cheese, ½ cup
(2 oz/60 g) freshly grated

Fresh basil, ¼ cup
(1 oz/30 g) slivered

SERVES 4–6

1 Roast the eggplant

Preheat the oven to 450°F (230°C). Brush the eggplant
slices with olive oil, season with salt and pepper, and place on
2 baking sheets. Roast, turning once, until the slices are nicely
browned, about 20 minutes total.

2 Layer the eggplant

Meanwhile, in a saucepan over medium heat, warm the
Bolognese sauce. Reduce the oven temperature to 375°F
(190°C). Spread the bottom of a 10-by-12-inch (25-by-30-cm)
baking dish with a large spoonful of the sauce. Lay one-third
of the eggplant slices on the bottom of the dish, overlapping
them slightly. Top with 1 cup (8 fl oz/250 ml) of the sauce
and one-third of the mozzarella slices. Repeat to make 2 more
layers. Sprinkle the Parmesan on top.

3 Bake the eggplant

Bake the eggplant lasagna until warmed through and
the cheese is melted, about 20 minutes. Remove from the oven
and let stand for 10 minutes. Serve, garnished with the basil.

cook's tip

If you can only find large
eggplants, sprinkle the slices
with coarse salt on both sides
and place in a colander set
over a plate. Let drain for about
30 minutes before roasting.
The eggplant can be roasted
or grilled a day in advance and
refrigerated until ready to use.

cook's tip

To stuff cannelloni easily, spoon the filling into a large, heavy-duty resealable plastic bag. Push the filling down into one corner of the bag, forcing out any air at the same time. Twist the bag several times where the filling ends. Then, snip off the corner of the bag with scissors and squeeze the filling through the hole into the cannelloni.

stuffed cannelloni with bolognese

1 Cook the pasta

Bring a large pot of water to a boil. Add 2 tablespoons salt and the pasta. Cook, stirring occasionally to prevent sticking, until not quite al dente, about 2 minutes less than the package directions. Drain the pasta, rinse under cool water to prevent sticking, and set aside.

2 Prepare the filling

Put the spinach and ½ cup (4 fl oz/125 ml) water in a large frying pan over medium heat. Cook, stirring frequently, until wilted, about 2 minutes. Drain, pressing on the spinach with the back of a large spoon to remove as much water as possible. In a large bowl, combine the spinach, ricotta, egg yolks, nutmeg, ½ teaspoon salt, ¼ teaspoon pepper, and half of the Parmesan. Blend well with a wooden spoon.

3 Stuff and bake the cannelloni

Preheat the oven to 375°F (190°C). Spread the bottom of a 10-by-12-inch (25-by-30-cm) baking dish with a large spoonful of the sauce. Using a teaspoon, stuff the cannelloni with the spinach filling. Place the stuffed pasta in the dish and spoon the sauce over the top. Sprinkle with the remaining Parmesan and cover with aluminum foil. Bake for 15 minutes. Remove the foil and bake until bubbly and nicely colored, about 10 minutes longer. Remove the cannelloni from the oven and let cool for 10–15 minutes before serving.

Bolognese Sauce (page 80), 4 cups (32 fl oz/1 l)

Salt and freshly ground pepper

Cannelloni pasta, ½ lb (250 g)

Baby spinach, 1½ lb (750 g), coarsely chopped

Fresh ricotta, 3 cups (1½ lb/750 g)

Egg yolks, 2, lightly beaten

Ground nutmeg, ¼ teaspoon

Parmesan cheese, 1 cup (4 oz/125 g) freshly grated

SERVES 4–6

turkey breast in mole

Olive oil, 3 tablespoons

Yellow onions, 2, chopped

Slivered almonds, ½ cup
(2½ oz/75 g)

Chile powder, 1 tablespoon

Ground cumin, 1 teaspoon

Ground cinnamon,
½ teaspoon

Diced tomatoes, 1 can
(14½ oz/455 g), drained

Bittersweet chocolate,
¼ cup (1½ oz/45 g),
chopped

Dried oregano, 1 teaspoon

**Salt and freshly ground
pepper**

Chicken broth, 2 cups
(16 fl oz/500 ml)

**Bone-in turkey breast
halves,** 2, about 4 lb (2 kg)
total weight, skin removed

SERVES 4

makes about 12 cups (6 lb/
3 kg) turkey mole total

This streamlined version of Mexican mole gains
flavor from hours spent in the slow cooker. Serve
it with rice for dinner tonight, and save the rest
to make the recipes on the following pages.

1 Start the sauce
In a large frying pan over high heat, warm the oil. Add the
onions and almonds and sauté until just golden, 8–10 minutes.
Stir in the chile powder, cumin, and cinnamon and sauté until
fragrant, about 30 seconds longer. Add the tomatoes, chocolate,
oregano, 2 teaspoons salt, 1 teaspoon pepper, and 1 cup
(8 fl oz/250 ml) of the broth and stir until the chocolate has
melted, about 1 minute.

2 Cook the sauce and turkey
In a food processor or blender, process the mole
mixture, in batches if necessary, to a smooth purée. Return the
purée to the frying pan over medium-high heat. Add the
remaining 1 cup broth and bring to a simmer. Place the turkey
breast halves in the slow cooker and pour the sauce over
them. Cover and cook on the high-heat setting for 4 hours
or the low-heat setting for 8 hours.

3 Finish the dish
Transfer the breast halves to a cutting board. Using
a sharp knife, cut one turkey breast into slices. Arrange the slices
on a platter. Spoon the mole over the top, and serve. Let
the other turkey breast half cool, then store for later use (see
Storage Tip, right).

storage tip

Let the mole cool to room temperature. With your fingers or a pair of forks, shred the meat to use in the recipes that follow. Stir together the shredded turkey with the remaining mole, then transfer to airtight containers and store in the refrigerator for up to 2 days or in the freezer for up to 1 month.

cook's tip

For an easy variation, make soft tacos by warming the corn tortillas as described in the recipe and reheating the mole mixture separately in a saucepan over medium heat. Spoon the hot turkey mole into each tortilla, passing the cheese, sour cream, and avocado slices at the table.

mole
enchiladas

1 Soften the tortillas
Preheat the oven to 375°F (190°C). Warm a heavy frying pan over medium heat. One at a time, soften the tortillas by placing them in the pan for about 15 seconds on each side, taking care not to burn them.

2 Prepare the enchiladas
Lightly oil a baking dish large enough to hold 8 enchiladas side by side. Set aside about ¼ cup (2 fl oz/60 ml) of the mole (without turkey) and enough cheese to use for topping the enchiladas. Spread a scant ½ cup (4 fl oz/125 ml) of the turkey mole down the center of a tortilla, sprinkle the filling with about 3 tablespoons of the cheese, roll up the tortilla, and place it seam side down in the dish. Repeat until you have formed all 8 enchiladas. Drizzle the reserved sauce over the top of the enchiladas and sprinkle with the remaining cheese.

3 Bake the enchiladas
Bake the enchiladas until the filling is bubbling and the cheese is melted and golden, about 20 minutes. Carefully transfer 2 enchiladas each to 4 plates, garnish with the sour cream and avocado slices, and serve.

Turkey Breast in Mole (page 88), 4 cups (2 lb/ 1 kg), meat shredded

Corn tortillas, 8

Canola oil, for greasing

Monterey jack cheese, ½ cup (8 oz/250 g) shredded

Sour cream, 6 tablespoons (3 oz/90 g)

Avocado, 1, halved, pitted, peeled, and sliced

SERVES 4

mole huevos rancheros

Turkey Breast in Mole (page 88), 4 cups (2 lb/ 1 kg), with meat shredded

Unsalted butter, 6 tablespoons (3 oz/90 g)

Corn tortillas, 8

Eggs, 8

Salt and freshly ground pepper

Tomato salsa, 1 cup (8 oz/250 g), plus more for serving

Queso fresco or **Monterey jack cheese,** 6 oz (185 g), crumbled or shredded

Sour cream, 6 tablespoons (3 oz/90 g)

Avocado, 1, halved, pitted, peeled, and sliced

SERVES 4

1 Prepare the ingredients

Preheat the broiler (grill). In a saucepan over medium heat, warm the turkey and mole sauce, stirring occasionally, until hot, 5–7 minutes. Meanwhile, in a large frying pan over medium-low heat, melt the butter. Remove the pan from the heat. Using a basting brush, lightly brush each tortilla on both sides with a little of the melted butter and place on a rimmed baking sheet in a single layer. Place the tortillas under the broiler and broil (grill), turning once, until golden brown and crisp on both sides, 2–3 minutes on each side. Watch closely, as they can burn easily. Place 2 tortillas each on 4 plates.

2 Cook the eggs

Return the frying pan with the butter to medium heat. When the butter is hot, carefully break each egg into the pan and sprinkle with salt and pepper. Cook until the whites are opaque and the yolks are done to your liking, about 5 minutes for cooked but still-runny yolks. As the eggs cook, baste them by spooning the butter in the pan over the tops.

3 Finish the dish

Spoon the warm turkey mole over the tortillas on each plate. Transfer 2 fried eggs to each plate and garnish each egg with the salsa, cheese, and sour cream and avocado. Serve, passing additional salsa at the table.

cook's tip

If you prefer, you can scramble
the eggs. Break the eggs into
a bowl, beat until frothy with a
fork, and season lightly with salt
and pepper. Cook the eggs in
the butter, stirring frequently,
until they form soft curds.

the smarter cook

Smart cooking is all about simple ideas that help you put together delicious meals without spending all day in the kitchen. Building a meal around a one-pot dish that you assemble in the morning and cook during the day is one of the smartest ways to minimize kitchen time. The recipes in this book are the starting point for getting dinner on the table, especially on weeknights when you're pressed for time.

Keep your panty well stocked, and you have the foundation for your weeknight meals. Plan your meals, and you'll make fewer trips to the store. Cook up a big batch of Ratatouille or Bolognese Sauce one night, and use it in other recipes during the week or in the future. In the following pages, you'll find tips on how to manage your time and stock your kitchen—the keys to becoming a smarter cook.

slow cooking

Introduced in 1971 by the Rival Company, the slow cooker was originally designed as an electric bean cooker. But it soon proved to be an efficient vessel for cooking such dishes as braises and stews that rely on moist heat, rather than the roasts and baked dishes that cook in the dry heat of an oven. Plus, once the slow cooker was turned on, the cook was free until dinnertime.

The countertop appliance, dubbed the Crock-Pot®, was initially marketed to working women who were too busy to cook, but still wanted to put a home-cooked meal on the family table. It wasn't long, however, before its popularity transformed it into an essential piece of equipment in kitchens everywhere. The original machine's beige and avocado-green styling captured the expression of the era so completely that it eventually began to look dated. Even the concept of plugging in a machine that cooks a stew while you run errands or go to work took on a feeling of nostalgia. Yet because of its convenience, economy, and practicality, the slow cooker never disappeared, and eventually the arrival of updated models—along with the reemergence of such comfort foods as slow braises and stews—put the appliance back in the kitchens of modern cooks.

Today, slow cookers are manufactured by many companies, but they have similar components: an exterior metal casing with electric heating element and a glazed stoneware insert that is easy to remove and clean (in older models, inserts were not removable, which proved a hassle). Today's attractive vessels come in a variety of sizes, including small (1½–2½ qt/1.5–2.5 l), medium (3–4½ qt/3–4.5 l), and large (5–7 qt/5–7 l), as well as two shapes: the original round and the more recently introduced oval. The oval slow cooker is especially well suited to holding large cuts of meat, such as a whole chicken or a beef brisket. All the recipes in this book were made in a 7-qt (7-l) oval slow cooker.

Contemporary slow cookers offer new features that provide increased convenience. For example, some programmable models continuously display the remaining cooking time so you can plan your dinnertime, and will automatically switch to the warm setting once the cooking time is up.

THE RECIPES IN THIS BOOK

All of the recipes in this book were tested in a 7-quart (7-liter) oval-shaped slow cooker. If you have a 3½-quart (3.5-liter) slow cooker, halve the recipes.

Many recipes call for browning meat before adding it to the pot. Although it is an extra step, it imparts a deep flavor and rich color to the dish. You can skip this step if you are pressed for time, but the results will be inferior.

Each recipe in this book provides two options for cooking times. Which you choose will depend on whether you want to use the high or the low setting on your slow cooker. If you plan to start the slow cooker and leave for the day, the low temperature setting is recommended. Generally, the low setting, which produces a gentle simmer, also results in more tender meat and concentrated flavor.

For the best results, fill the slow cooker no more than half to two-thirds full.

Do not allow leftovers to sit in the slow cooker for more than 2 hours after cooking. Transfer them to an airtight container and store in the refrigerator or freezer (page 106).

Once you have chosen your slow-cooker recipe or recipes for the week, give some thought to organizing your time. The more you can do in advance, the more quickly and easily the meal will come together at dinnertime.

stock up Keep the pantry stocked, checking regularly to see what you have and replenishing as needed, so the basic nonperishable ingredients are always on hand when you want to make your favorite slow-cooker dishes.

shop less If you have made a weekly meal plan, you will probably need to shop only two or three times a week for fresh ingredients like produce or meat.

do it ahead Do whatever you can ahead of time. The ingredients for most of the recipes can be prepared in the evening and then assembled the next day. This can mean browning meat in advance or gathering the ingredients you need the night before to make morning prep go quickly. Keep meat and chopped vegetables in separate containers if you're storing them overnight.

cook smarter Before you begin, take a few minutes to reread the recipe and to assemble your equipment and prep your ingredients. If possible, enlist family members to help you with assembly and clean up.

double up When planning a week's worth of dinners, look for opportunities to utilize one night's leftovers, such as turkey mole, in other recipes like tacos, enchiladas, or huevos rancheros.

use the slow cooker with success

■ The two keys to safe cooking in the slow cooker are maintaining a consistent temperature and following recommended cooking times.

■ Unless a recipe specifies otherwise, always thaw frozen foods before adding them to the slow cooker to prevent compromising the internal temperature of the vessel. Frozen foods can lower the cooking temperature to a level that allows for unsafe bacterial growth.

■ Cooking large pieces of meat in the wrong-sized slow cooker can also lead to unsafe bacterial growth. Always use the slow cooker size recommended in the recipe to ensure the meat cooks through.

■ It is sometimes necessary to lift the lid on the slow cooker, such as when you add ingredients halfway through cooking or when you check for doneness. Try to avoid doing this too often, however. It allows steam to escape, lowering the overall cooking temperature inside the pot.

■ If you return home while the cooker is going and find that the power has gone out in your absence, discard the contents of the slow cooker even if it looks done. There is no way to know whether the food has cooked safely and thoroughly.

■ When loading the pot, fill it with solid ingredients first, placing those that take longer to cook, such as meat or potatoes, on the bottom. Place the crock in the base and then add any liquid, to protect against spillage.

■ The lid of the slow cooker can become hot during cooking, so always handle it with care, opening it away from you to avoid a blast of steam and using protective oven mitts.

■ Never subject your slow cooker's stoneware insert to extreme changes in temperature. For example, do not put it in the freezer or set it over direct heat on the stove top. Also, never refrigerate leftovers in the insert; instead, transfer them to another container for storage.

■ The glazed surface of the pot is easy to clean. Use soap and water and avoid abrasives. Also, never use cold water if the pot is still hot.

get started

With a little planning and a well-organized kitchen, you can become a smarter cook who regularly turns out delicious slow-cooker dishes with ease. Three simple strategies will make it possible: drawing up a weekly meal plan, figuring out when to fit cooking into your busy schedule, and keeping your pantry and refrigerator stocked with basic items (pages 104–107).

plan a slow-cooked meal

Get into the habit of putting together a weekly meal plan, which can take the worry out of what to cook for dinner and provide make-ahead opportunities that will save you time when you need it most. (See Round It Out to the right and Sample Meals on page 100 for ideas.) Once you have settled on your menus, you can put together a list of fresh ingredients you need to buy in order to make the recipes.

- **A slow-cooked dish is the perfect anchor for a meal.** Whether you're preparing a beef stew, a hearty soup, or a vegetable curry, it will be flavorful, filling, and easy to cook, serve, store, and reheat. Stews and braises are typically relegated to the weekend, when you can stay close to the stove for several hours. The slow cooker allows these savory dishes to become a more convenient dinner solution. Use this book to build a repertoire of reliable favorites that you and your family can enjoy on a regular basis.

- **Plan seasonally.** While you can make all of the dishes in this book at any time, cooking with fresh seasonal ingredients is an easy way to guarantee great flavor and to enjoy meals that match the time of year, both the weather and the mood. To the right is a guide to using the best that the season has to offer whenever you are in the kitchen. You'll enjoy better flavors, and you'll probably save money, too, because in-season ingredients are often less expensive. Pick recipes that fit the weather: most of these recipes are for hearty, warming dishes perfect for autumn and winter, but some are perfect for summer parties and picnics, when a large batch of Ratatouille or Pulled Pork is always welcome.

THINK SEASONALLY

spring Make lightly flavored soups, braises, and stews that feature delicate spring produce and other ingredients, such as asparagus, beets, fava (broad) beans, fennel, herbs (dill, chives, parsley, mint), green garlic, green (spring) onions, new potatoes, peas, and lamb.

summer Focus on simple dishes that showcase the best of the harvest, such as avocados, bell peppers (capsicums), chiles, corn, cucumbers, eggplants (aubergines), green beans, herbs (basil, thyme, parsley), tomatoes, and zucchini (courgettes) and other summer squashes.

autumn Prepare substantial, warming meat braises or soups made with the season's root vegetables and other ingredients, like apples, broccoli, leeks, butternut squashes, cauliflower, fresh and dried herbs (bay leaves, sage, rosemary), mushrooms, potatoes, and yams.

winter Cook warming stews and spicy curries that call for meat, hearty winter vegetables, and other fresh seasonal ingredients, such as beets, cabbage, chard, fresh herbs (sage, rosemary), kale, wild and cultivated mushrooms, rutabagas, turnips, and winter squashes.

round it out

Once you have decided what dish to make as the centerpiece of your meal, choose from among a wide variety of appealing side dishes to round out the menu. Keep in mind both speed and ease of preparation.

steamed rice Aromatic basmati rice and jasmine rice are long-grain varieties that work especially well as accompaniments to slow-cooked dishes.

couscous A staple in North African cooking, couscous is tiny pasta beads made from coarsely milled semolina. Precooked dried couscous, sometimes called instant or quick-cooking couscous, is available either packaged or in bulk. It requires only rehydrating in boiling water before serving. You can offer it plain, or you can add raisins, currants, toasted nuts, or fresh herbs.

mashed potatoes Fluffy mashed potatoes are perfect for soaking up the fragrant juices of slow-cooked meats such as braised lamb chops. Yukon gold and russet are both good choices for making mashed potatoes.

egg noodles Egg noodles are a natural match for many slow-cooked dishes. Follow the cooking directions on the package if you buy dried egg noodles, or save time by purchasing fresh egg noodles, such as fettuccine, which are available at many upscale markets and well-stocked supermarkets, and cook in 2 to 3 minutes. Pasta should always be cooked al dente—tender yet with some firmness at the center.

polenta This Italian cornmeal is traditionally prepared by pouring it slowly into boiling water and stirring constantly with a wooden spoon for at least 30 minutes. Instant polenta is cooked the same way, but takes much less time because the grains have already been parboiled. You can also find tubes of cooked polenta in most well-stocked supermarkets. They can be sliced and baked, fried, or grilled.

artisanal bread Warm briefly in the oven, if desired, then slice and serve in a napkin-lined basket with butter or extra-virgin olive oil. Consider artisanal rolls, too, which are an ideal base for serving up such slow-cooked dishes as Pulled Pork.

corn bread Warm slices of store-bought corn bread in the oven or toaster oven. Or, make your own using a mix or from scratch; add frozen corn kernels for texture and flavor. Serve alongside braised meats or chili.

salad Buy prewashed greens to save time. Choose salad ingredients that complement the dish you are serving, such as pairing a simple salad of mixed baby greens with autumnal Pork Loin with Apples and Sage, or a fresh Caesar salad with the Mediterranean-inspired Tuscan Ribollita.

fresh vegetables Some slow-cooker dishes include an array of fresh vegetables; others are simply large cuts of braised meat that will benefit from a side dish of steamed, sautéed, or roasted seasonal vegetables. Or, consider a room-temperature vegetable dish, such as green beans dressed with a vinaigrette, that can be prepared ahead.

tomatoes Slice flavorful in-season tomatoes, arrange on a platter, and season with olive oil, salt, and pepper. If desired, top with crumbled feta cheese, olives, or chopped fresh herbs.

crostini Spread toasted baguette rounds with store-bought spreads, such as tapenade, hummus, or roasted red pepper (capsicum) spread. Serve as a starter or offer as accompaniments to soups or stews.

make it easy

- **Prep** Use a food processor to make quick work of chopping vegetables. Prep vegetables for two meals: when you're chopping vegetables for one dinner, chop extra vegetables and store them in an airtight container in the refrigerator to use the next night.

- **Sauté** Many of the recipes in this book begin with sautéing aromatic vegetables (onions, carrots, celery) and seasonings in butter or oil to create a flavorful base for whatever dish you're preparing. Sauté these in advance and store in an airtight container in the refrigerator.

- **Brown** In many cases, browning meat or poultry before you add it to the slow cooker will result in a dish that looks and tastes better. Browning is an easy process. Simply put the meat or poultry in a large frying pan over medium-high heat and turn it as needed until it is richly colored on all sides. Then, using tongs or a slotted spoon, transfer the browned meat or poultry to the slow cooker.

- **Deglaze** Some recipes call for deglazing the pan after browning the meat or poultry. To do so, remove the meat from the pan, leaving behind the drippings and browned bits. Place the pan over medium-high heat and pour in broth, wine, or another liquid. As the liquid boils, stir, scraping up the browned bits from the pan bottom, and then add the contents of the pan to the slow cooker.

- **Purée** The slow cooker is ideal for making puréed soups, and a blender is the most efficient tool for puréeing. Fill the blender no more than two-thirds full with the hot soup. (You usually need to work in batches.) Cover with the lid, making sure it is secure, and then drape a kitchen towel over the lid in case there is splattering. Hold the lid down with one hand, and gradually increase the speed as necessary. A food processor or immersion blender, which can be used directly in the stoneware insert, can also be used.

- **Season** Remove a small amount of the finished dish from the slow cooker, taste, season with salt and pepper, and taste again. This gives you an idea of how much seasoning to add, so you don't overseason the pot.

sample meals

These sample meals include a recipe suggestion and accompaniments that can be put together quickly.

Indian Vegetable Curry
(page 13)

Steamed basmati rice

Purchased samosas & chutney

Chile Verde
(page 21)

Warm corn tortillas

Pinto beans

Butternut Squash Soup
(page 32)

Spinach salad with bacon
& honey-mustard vinaigrette

**Pork Roast with
Dried-Fruit Compote**
(page 47)

Mashed potatoes

Sautéed spinach

**Sausages with
Ratatouille**
(page 69)

Roasted new potatoes with rosemary

Roasted Eggplant Lasagna
(page 84)

Mixed salad greens with red wine
vinaigrette

Crusty bread

keep it edible Avoid garnishes such as woody herb sprigs that look attractive but cannot be easily eaten.

reserve ingredients during prep While preparing a dish, save some of the fresh ingredients, such as minced herbs or sour cream, to use for garnishing.

make it simple Use no more than 1 or 2 garnishes for both better flavor and a nicer presentation.

keep it light Use only a small amount of any ingredient for garnishing, and choose ingredients that will remain on the surface, rather than sink into the dish.

EASY GARNISHES

sour cream or plain yogurt Thin with milk and drizzle over the dish; ideal for curries and puréed soups.

parmesan cheese Grate directly onto each serving for the best flavor, or form curls using a vegetable peeler.

fresh chives Snip with scissors directly onto each serving.

fresh herbs Strip leaves from stems and then roughly chop if necessary.

extra-virgin olive oil Drizzle good-quality olive oil over each serving.

lemon Cut into wedges and use as a garnish for Italian-inspired dishes like Grilled Flank Steak with White Beans.

shortcut ingredients

Whatever you are cooking, certain ingredients can make the job easier and save prep time, either because they are precooked or because they add concentrated, intense flavor. Here are some that are particularly useful when you are using your slow cooker.

- **Canned beans** Prepared beans will save you soaking and simmering time. Discard the liquid and rinse beans well before using. Add the beans to the slow cooker toward the end of cooking to retain their texture.

- **Rotisserie-cooked chicken** Buy enough chicken for dinner one night, plus leftovers, and cut up the leftover meat to add to a simple dish from the slow cooker the next night. Add the chicken toward the end of the cooking time to prevent it from toughening.

- **Cooked sausages** Slice fully cooked sausages, such as andouille, smoked chorizo, chicken with apple, or kielbasa, and add directly to dishes such as White Bean Soup, or brown first for extra flavor.

- **Frozen vegetables** Keep a supply of frozen peas, pearl onions, and corn on hand for sprucing up a variety of dishes.

- **Canned tomatoes** Canned tomatoes don't need to be peeled, require a shorter cooking time, and are more flavorful than out-of-season tomatoes.

- **Dried mushrooms** The concentrated flavor of dried porcini, shiitake, or other mushrooms complements soups, braises, and stews. To reconstitute, place mushrooms in a heatproof bowl, cover with boiling water, cover the bowl, and soak until soft and flexible, at least 10 minutes. Remove the mushrooms, squeezing out the excess liquid into the bowl. Chop the mushrooms (or cut as desired), removing and discarding any woody stems. The soaking liquid can also be added to the slow cooker. To remove any grit before using, strain it through a fine-mesh sieve lined with cheesecloth (muslin) or a coffee filter.

- **Tomato paste** Buy good-quality tomato paste in a tube, which, once opened, can be kept in the refrigerator for several months. Add a small amount to tomato-based dishes to intensify flavor.

the well-stocked kitchen

Smart cooking is all about being prepared. Keeping your pantry, refrigerator, and freezer well stocked and organized means you'll save time when you are ready to cook. Get into the habit of keeping track of what is in your kitchen, and you'll find you can shop less frequently.

Here's a guide to the essential ingredients to have on hand for making dishes in the slow cooker, along with tips and ideas on how to keep them fresh and in order. Use it to take stock of what's in your kitchen now so that you know what you need to buy or replace. The time you spend taking inventory is an investment that will pay off whenever you need to put dinner on the table. Once your pantry, refrigerator, and freezer are stocked, you'll be able to make any recipe in this book by buying just a few fresh ingredients.

the pantry

The pantry is usually a cupboard or two or a closet in which you store such nonperishable items as dried herbs and spices, dried fruits, dried pastas and grains, and canned and bottled goods, as well as such staple fresh ingredients as garlic, yellow onions, and potatoes. It should be relatively cool, dry, and dark, and should be away from the stove, as cooking heat can hasten spoilage.

stock your pantry

- Take inventory of what is in your pantry using the Pantry Staples list.

- Remove everything from the pantry; clean the shelves and reline with paper, if needed; and then re-sort the items by type.

- Discard items that have passed their expiration date or have a stale or otherwise questionable appearance.

- Make a list of items that you need to replace or stock.

- Shop for the items on your list.

- Restock the pantry, organizing items by type so everything is easy to find.

- Write the purchase date on perishable items and clearly label bulk items.

- Keep staples you use often toward the front of the pantry.

- Keep dried herbs and spices in separate containers and preferably in a separate spice or herb organizer, shelf, or drawer.

keep it organized

- Look over the recipes in your weekly menu plan and check your pantry to make sure you have all the ingredients you'll need.

- Rotate items as you use them, moving the oldest ones to the front of the pantry so they will be used first.

- Keep a list of the items you use up so that you can replace them.

PANTRY STORAGE

dried herbs & spices These dried ingredients start losing their potency after about 6 months. Buy them in small quantities and store in airtight containers.

oils Light and heat are enemies of olive oil, so store oil in a cool, dark place, in tightly corked or capped dark glass bottles. Although oils will keep for up to a year, their flavor diminishes over time. Once opened, store for 3 months at room temperature or in the refrigerator for up to 6 months. Taste or smell oils to make sure they are not rancid before using.

canned foods Discard canned foods if the can shows any signs of expansion or buckling. Once you have opened a can, transfer the unused contents to an airtight container and refrigerate or freeze.

grains & pastas Store in airtight glass or plastic containers, checking occasionally for signs of infestation or rancidity.

fresh pantry items Store in a cool, dark place with plenty of air, checking occasionally for signs of sprouting or spoilage. Never put potatoes alongside onions; when placed next to each other, they produce gases that hasten spoilage.

GRAINS, PASTAS & DRIED LEGUMES

cannellini or other small white beans

cannelloni pasta

corn tortillas

country bread

couscous

egg noodles

fettuccine

green split peas

lentils

long-grain rice

penne

polenta

soft sandwich rolls

spaghetti

FRESH FOODS

avocados

garlic

lemons

limes

potatoes

red onions

shallots

sweet potatoes

white onions

yellow onions

SPIRITS

ale or dark beer

dry white wine

full-bodied red wine

port

PACKAGED FOODS

beef broth

cannellini beans (canned)

chicken broth

chickpeas (garbanzo beans)

chipotle chiles in adobo sauce

coconut milk

crushed plum (Roma) tomatoes

green olives

roasted whole green chiles

soy sauce

tomato ketchup

tomato paste

tomato salsa

vegetable broth

whole plum (Roma) tomatoes

Worcestershire sauce

OILS & VINEGARS

canola oil

cider vinegar

corn oil

olive oil

red wine vinegar

rice vinegar

DRIED HERBS & SPICES

bay leaves

black peppercorns

cayenne pepper

chili powder

cinnamon sticks

coarse salt (kosher or sea salt)

coriander seeds

cumin seeds

dried sage

dry mustard

filé powder

ground coriander

ground cumin

ground cinnamon

ground ginger

ground nutmeg

ground turmeric

ground white pepper

oregano

paprika

red pepper flakes

thyme

DRIED FRUITS

dried apricots

dried figs

pitted prunes

MISCELLANEOUS

bittersweet chocolate

cornstarch (cornflour)

dark brown sugar

flour

gingersnap cookies

granulated sugar

light brown sugar

light molasses

slivered blanched almonds

unsweetened shredded dried coconut

the refrigerator & freezer

Once you have stocked and organized your pantry, you can apply the same time-saving principles to your refrigerator and freezer. Used for short-term cold storage, the refrigerator is ideal for storing your meats, poultry, vegetables, and leftovers. Done properly, freezing will preserve most of the flavor and nutrients in braises, stews, and certain soups.

general tips

- Foods lose flavor under refrigeration, so proper storage and an even temperature of below 40°F (5°C) is important.

- Freeze foods at 0°F (-18°C) or below to retain color, texture, and flavor.

- Don't crowd foods in the refrigerator or freezer. Air should circulate freely to keep foods evenly cooled.

- To prevent freezer burn, use only moistureproof wrappings, such as aluminum foil, airtight plastic containers, or resealable plastic bags.

leftover storage

- Most dishes prepared in a slow cooker can be stored in the refrigerator for up to 4 days or in the freezer for up to 4 months.

- Check the contents of the refrigerator at least once a week and promptly discard old or spoiled food.

- Let food cool to room temperature before refrigerating or freezing. Transfer the cooled food to an airtight plastic or glass container, leaving room for expansion if freezing. Or, put the cooled food into a resealable plastic freezer bag, expelling as much air as possible before sealing.

- Plan on freezing some soups, stews, and braises in small batches for when you need to heat up just enough for 1 or 2 servings.

- Thaw frozen foods in the refrigerator or in the microwave. To avoid bacterial contamination, never thaw at room temperature.

KEEP IT ORGANIZED

clean first Remove items a few at a time and wash the refrigerator thoroughly with warm, soapy water, then rinse well with clear water. Wash and rinse your freezer at the same time.

rotate items Check the expiration dates on refrigerated items and discard any that have exceeded their time. Also, toss out any items that look questionable.

stock up Use the list on the opposite page as a starting point to decide what items you need to buy or replace.

shop Shop for the items on your list.

date of purchase Label items that you plan to keep for more than a few weeks, writing the date directly on the package or on a piece of masking tape.

WINE STORAGE

Once wine is uncorked, it is exposed to air, causing it to slowly oxidize and turn to vinegar. Store opened wine, tightly stoppered with a vacuum pump, in the refrigerator for no more 3 days.

fresh herb & vegetable storage

- Trim the stem ends of a bunch of parsley, stand the bunch in a glass of water, drape a plastic bag loosely over the leaves, and refrigerate. Wrap other fresh herbs in a damp paper towel, slip into a plastic bag, and store in the crisper. Rinse and stem all herbs just before using.

- Store tomatoes and eggplants (aubergines) at room temperature.

- Cut about ½ inch (12 mm) off the end of each asparagus spear, stand the spears, tips up, in a glass of cold water, and refrigerate, changing the water daily. The asparagus will keep for up to 1 week.

- Rinse leafy greens, such as kale, spin dry in a salad spinner, wrap in damp paper towels, and store in a resealable plastic bag in the crisper for up to 1 week. In general, store other vegetables in resealable bags in the crisper and rinse before using. Sturdy vegetables will keep for up to a week; more delicate ones will keep for only a few days.

meat & poultry storage

- Use fresh meat and poultry within 2 days of purchase. If buying packaged meats, check the expiration date and use before that date.

- Place packaged meats on a plate in the coldest part of the refrigerator. If only part of a package is used, discard the original wrapping and rewrap in fresh wrapping.

cheese & dairy storage

- Wrap all cheeses well to prevent them from drying out. Hard cheeses, such as Parmesan, have a low moisture content, so they keep longer than fresh cheeses, such as mozzarella and ricotta. Use fresh cheeses within a couple days. Store soft and semisoft cheeses for up to 2 weeks and hard cheeses for up to 1 month.

- Store dairy products in their original packaging. Check the expiration date and use before that date.

index

weldonowen

415 Jackson Street, Suite 200, San Francisco, CA 94111
www.wopublishing.com

MEALS IN MINUTES SERIES
Conceived and produced by Weldon Owen Inc.
Copyright © 2006 by Weldon Owen Inc. and Williams-Sonoma, Inc.

The recipes in this book have been previously published
as *Slow Cooker* in the Food Made Fast series.

All rights reserved, including the right of reproduction
in whole or in part in any form.

Color separations by Mission Productions in China
Printed by 1010 Printing in China

Set in Formata
This edition first printed in 2011
10 9 8 7 6 5 4 3 2

Library of Congress Cataloging-in-Publication
data is available.

Weldon Owen is a division of
BONNIER

Photographer Bill Bettencourt
Food Stylist Kevin Crafts
Photographer's Assistants Angelica Cao, Heidi Ladendorf
Food Stylist's Assistants Luis Bustamante, Alexa Hyman
Prop Stylist Leigh Nöe
Text Writer Kate Chynoweth

ACKNOWLEDGMENTS
Weldon Owen wishes to thank the following people
for their generous support in producing this book:
Davina Baum, Heather Belt, Ken DellaPenta, Judith Dunham,
Carolyn Miller, Marianne Mitten, Sharon Silva, Robin Turk,
Kate Washington, and Sharron Wood.

ISBN-13: 978-1-61628-156-4 (paperback)
ISBN-10: 1-61628-156-1

ISBN-13: 978-1-61628-176-2 (hardcover)
ISBN-10: 1-61628-176-6

A NOTE ON WEIGHTS AND MEASURES
All recipes include customary U.S. and metric measurements. Metric conversions are based on
a standard developed for these books and have been rounded off. Actual weights may vary.